TOPIC BOX

Houses and Homes

Rhoda Nottridge

Wayland

Titles in this series
Castles
Dinosaurs
Fairs and Circuses
Houses and Homes
Minibeasts
My Body
The Seasons
Transport

This book was prepared for Wayland (Publishers) Ltd
by Globe Education, Nantwich, Cheshire

Design concept by Pinpoint
Book design by Stephen Wheele Design
Artwork by Deborah Kindred

First published in 1996 by
Wayland (Publishers) Ltd
61 Western Road, Hove
East Sussex BN3 1JD

Printed and bound in Italy by
L. E. G. O. S.p.A., Vincenza

British Library Cataloguing in Publication Data

Nottridge, Rhoda
Houses and Homes. – (Topic Box Series)
I. Title II. Series
643.1

ISBN 0 7502 1607 7

Picture acknowledgements
Blacksmith Products 25, Bridgeman Art Library 7
Bruce Coleman 21 (Jennifer Fry), Eye Ubiquitous 8 (John D. Norman)
Life File 5 (Oleg Svyatoslavsky), 9 (Richard Powers), 13t (Jeremy Hoare), 13b (Sally Woodward), 14 (Selwyn Taylor),
15 (Barry Mayes), 16 (Emman Lee), 17 (Cecilia Innes), 18 (Emma Lee), 19(Vivienne Sharp), 22-23 (Emma Lee),
23 (Bob Harris), 26 (Andrew Wood), 27 (Emma Lee)
Robert Harding 20
Tony Stone 24 (Patrick Ward), 29t (Sue Cunningham), 29b (David Hanson)
Zefa 4, 10

Contents

Where Do You Live?

Everyone needs a home where they feel sheltered and safe. Your home is the place where you live.

When it is raining, you can stay dry at home. If it is cold outside you can keep warm at home. In hot countries, your home shelters you from the sun.

A home can be any kind of building – large or small. Some people even have homes on boats, in tents or in caravans that can be moved around.

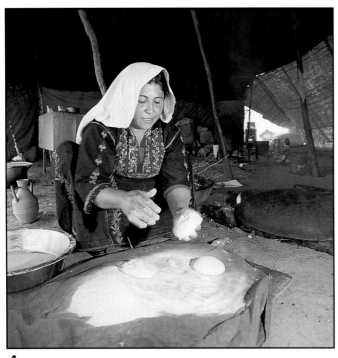

(Left) A tent is a home that you can put up anywhere.

(Left) These blocks of flats in Moscow provide many homes that keep people warm when it is cold outside.

Several houses are often built at the same time to make a new street.

Homes in History

In the past, people made their homes from materials they found nearby. When we look at different houses we can tell how old they are from the materials used and the way they were built.

Long ago, people did not have water in their homes and there were no electric lights. To keep warm they sometimes made fires inside their homes. With a fire they could also cook their food and heat water.

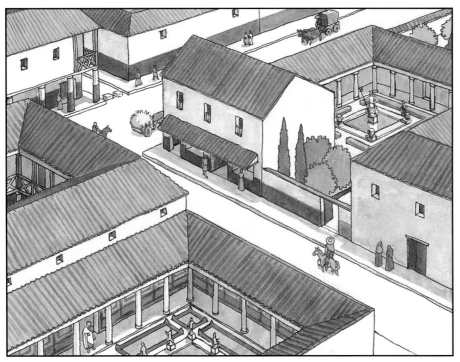

(Left) Wealthy Romans lived in well-built town houses. They also had villas in the country.

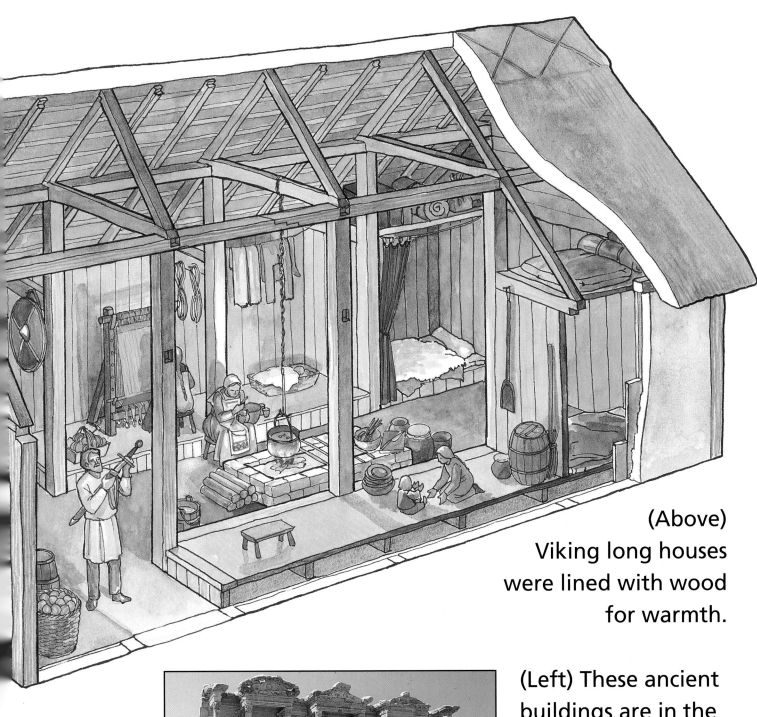

(Above)
Viking long houses
were lined with wood
for warmth.

(Left) These ancient
buildings are in the
city of Ephesus
which was once
home to 15,000
people. Today the
ruins of Ephesus are
in Turkey.

Shapes and Sizes

Around the world, people live in homes
of many shapes and sizes.

In some places, whole villages live together
with each family having a room in a big
house. In cities, friends often live together
and sometimes people live alone.

In the countryside, houses can be large
with plenty of space between, but in towns
and cities, the buildings are usually very
close together.

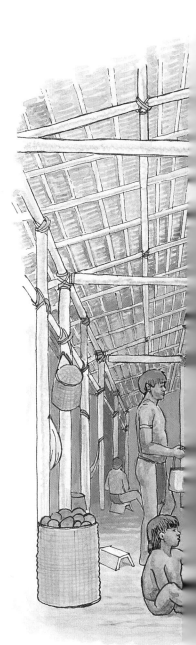

(Left) In hot countries like
Greece, houses are
sometimes built close
together. This shades
the street from the hot sun.

(Left) These houses in Syria are built in the shape of beehives. This keeps out the hot sun and the desert sand.

(Below) Long houses in the rainforest in Brazil are home to several families.

A Modern Home

Modern homes usually have rooms that are used for different activities – a kitchen for cooking, a dining room for eating, bathrooms for bathing, bedrooms for sleeping and living rooms where people can meet and relax together.

There is electricity for lighting. There are supplies of gas or oil for heating. Hot and cold water flows from the taps and dirty water disappears down the drains.

(Below) Kitchens are used for cooking.

bedroom

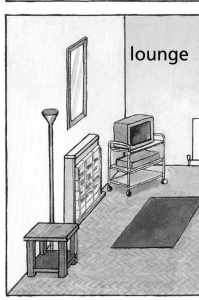

lounge

pipe brings in gas

wires bring in electricity

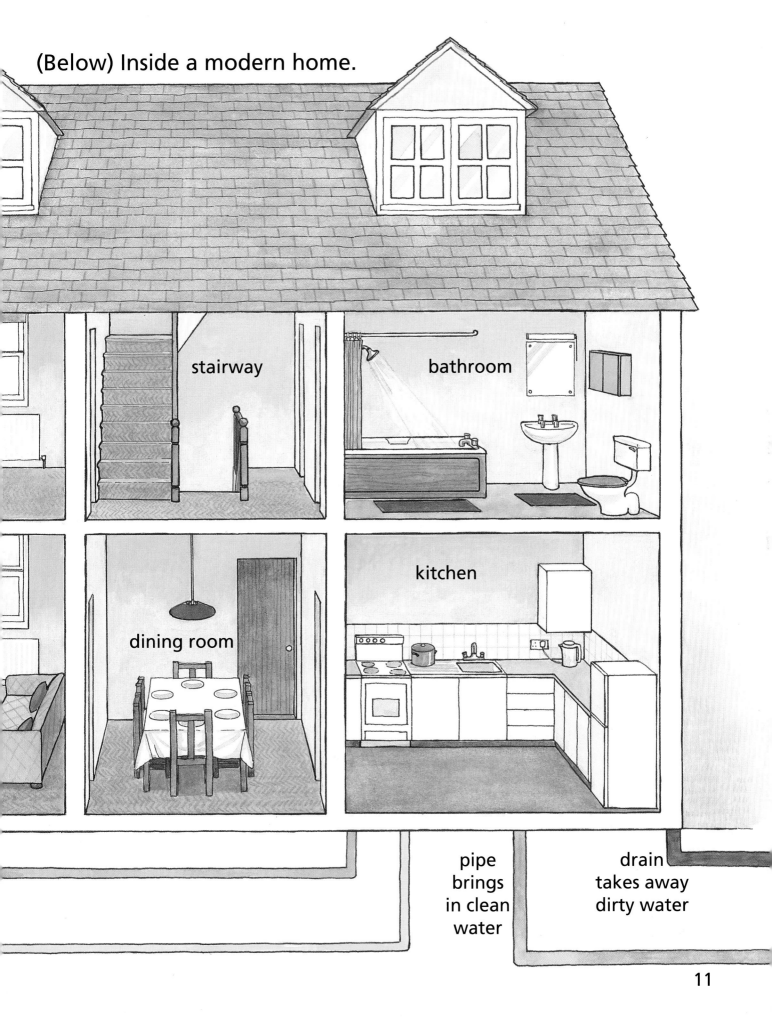

(Below) Inside a modern home.

stairway

bathroom

dining room

kitchen

pipe
brings
in clean
water

drain
takes away
dirty water

11

Wood, Grass and Mud

In countries where there are many trees, homes are often built from wood. Where strong grasses or bamboo grow, they can be woven together to make walls or roofs.

Mud can be used in dry, sunny places. It is baked hard by the hot sun and is made stronger when mixed with grass.

Where the weather is cold, earth and bark are used to make roofs. Grass and flowers take root and bloom.

Plan view.

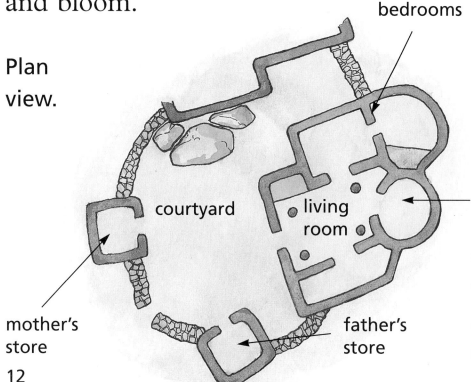

bedrooms

courtyard

living room

kitchen

mother's store

father's store

mother's store

courtyard

(Above) A Dogon village house, in Africa, is made with dried mud.

(Right) In south-east Asia, some houses are made of strong grass that is woven together.

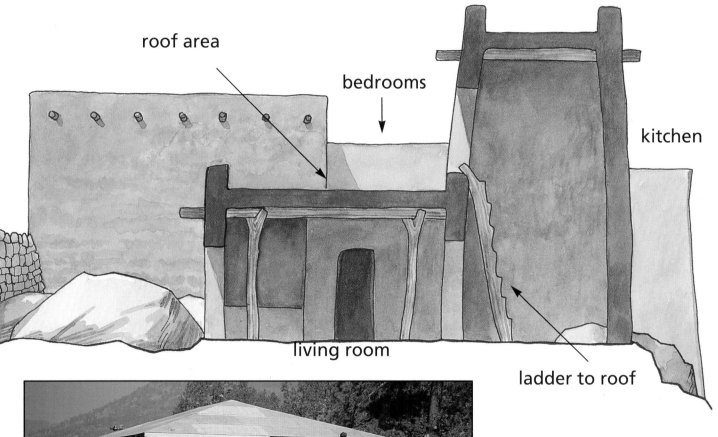

roof area

bedrooms

kitchen

living room

ladder to roof

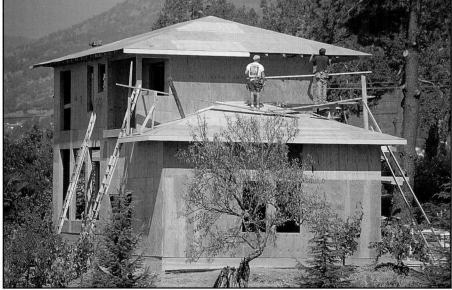

(Left) This house in North America is being built using local wood.

Stone, Brick and Steel

Bricks are made from a kind of mud called clay. Clay bricks are baked in a hot oven and become hard and almost waterproof. They are joined together with mortar – a mixture of sand, cement and water that sets hard.

Stone is a strong building material. Today it is often cut into small pieces and mixed with other lighter materials. Many tall buildings have a strong steel frame with panels of these lightweight materials in the gaps.

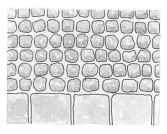

French stonework

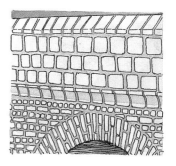

rusticated

(Left) These flats in Hong Kong have a steel frame. This helps to hold the building up and also makes it stronger.

14

(Left) In the Himalayan Mountains, there is plenty of stone for building houses.

(Left) Bricks and stones can be joined together in different ways to make strong walls.

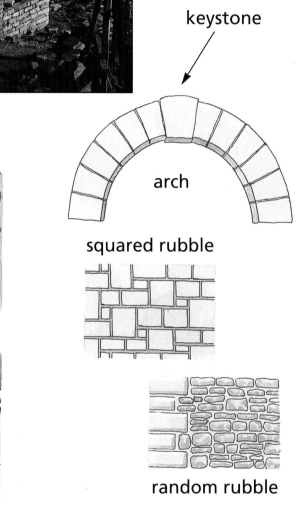

Mudéjar brickwork

herringbone

keystone

arch

squared rubble

random rubble

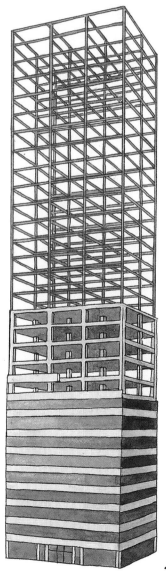

(Right) This is what the steel frame for a tall building looks like. Strong lightweight materials are fastened to the steel to make the walls.

Homes in Cold Places

People who live in the far north or high up in mountains need homes that keep them warm. Houses in cold places are often built of brick, stone or wood. These materials are strong enough to withstand bad weather.

Where snow falls in winter, roofs are sloped so the snow slips off easily. The walls are thick and small windows have shutters and two layers of glass. Inside heat comes from burning oil, gas, wood or coal.

double walls keep the heat inside

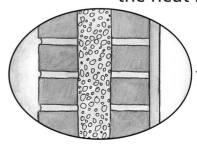

shutters keep out the cold

(Left) This Swiss house has a sloping roof so that the snow slides off easily.

16

(Right) Turf growing on the roofs of these houses in Sweden keeps them warm inside.

(Below) Keeping a house warm and safe.

the chimney takes away fumes

insulation stops heat going out through the roof

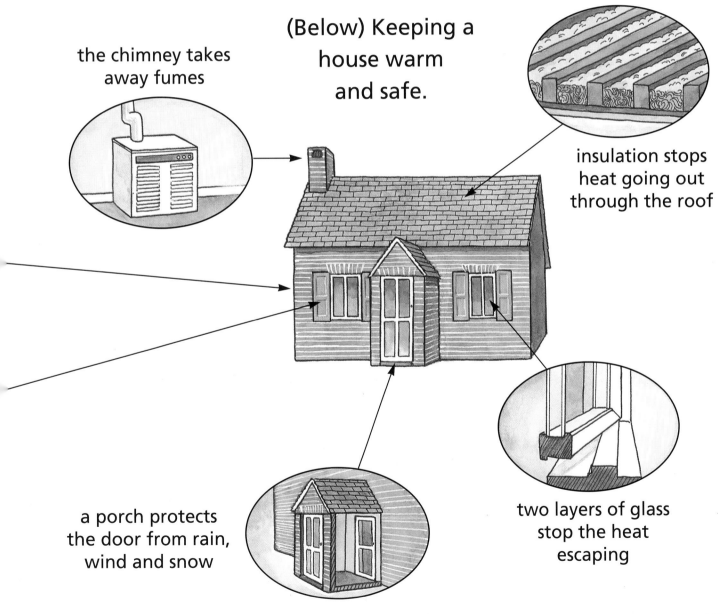

a porch protects the door from rain, wind and snow

two layers of glass stop the heat escaping

Homes in Hot Places

In hot countries, homes are built to keep out the heat of the sun. They have small windows so the sun cannot shine in. Balconies and verandas give shade and a place to sit in the cool of the evening.

In hot, rainy places, houses have big sloping roofs so heavy rain runs off easily. Often houses are raised from the ground keeping rainwater out, and allowing air to flow beneath to keep the houses cool.

(Left) The houses in this Moroccan village are cool inside.

(Right) The veranda of this Australian home shades it from the sun.

These houses in Indonesia have huge roofs that keep out the hot sun and allow heavy monsoon rain to run off.

Mobile Homes

A mobile home is one that can be moved around – usually a tent or a caravan. Some people move because they have animals that feed in different places depending on the season. Other people just like to wander from place to place.

Caravans can be towed by a car or truck, but large ones usually stay in one place on a caravan site. Some are holiday homes but many are lived in all the year round.

(Below) People who travel with their animals in Mongolia build tents called yurts to live in.

(Left) This is the kind of caravan that gypsies in Europe used to have as their homes. They were very beautifully painted.

(Right) Kurdish nomads in Iran live in low black tents with open sides to keep them cool.

Homes on Water

Wherever there are inland waterways or sheltered harbours, people can be found living in boats. Usually the boats have a mooring where they stay most of the time.

Where the weather is hot and steamy, houses are sometimes built on stilts over water. The water is cooler than the land, so it keeps the houses cool. The houses are connected to the land by bridges and the stilts protect the houses from flooding.

(Right) In south-east Asia where it is very hot and rain falls often, some homes are built on stilts by river banks.

(Left) A European canal boat makes a very comfortable home.

(Below) These boats in Hong Kong harbour are the only homes their owners have. There is no room for them on land.

Castles and Mansions

In the past rich and important people built strong castles to keep their families safe. The castles were built on the tops of hills or had moats to keep people out. The walls were high and a drawbridge protected the entrance.

Today we have different ways of protecting our houses. Steel gates with electronic locks make entry difficult. High fences are not easy to climb. Video cameras keep watch and alarms ring if intruders enter.

(Left) The White House is the home of the president of the USA. The president has a very important job. The White House is protected to make it safe.

(Left) People who need to feel very safe in their homes have special gates with electronic locks. The gates only open for visitors allowed in.

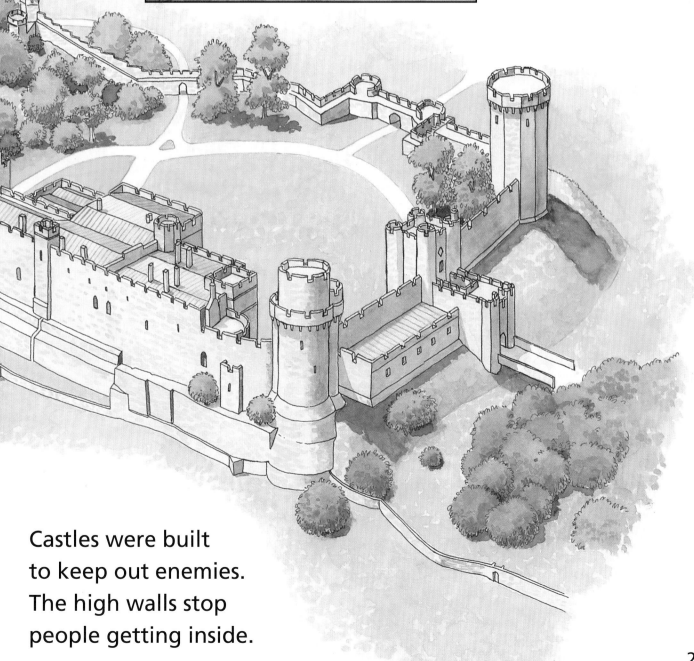

Castles were built to keep out enemies. The high walls stop people getting inside.

Inside a Home

People decorate and furnish their homes to make them comfortable to live in. A room decorated in bright colours feels different from the same room decorated in dull colours. Carpets and thick curtains keep houses warm. Stone floors and venetian blinds keep them cool.

Different people feel comfortable in different surroundings. The way a home looks tells you about the people living there.

Different kinds of windows.

in north Africa, some old windows have attractive metal bars

(Right) A mosaic is a floor decoration made of hundreds of pieces of coloured stone. This one was built by Roman craftsmen in Portugal.

many modern
windows are
double-glazed

some old European
windows have
stone frames

sash windows
slide up and down

French windows
open like doors

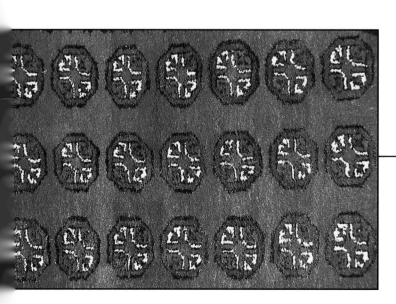

(Left) Some of the patterns
woven into carpets have special
meanings. This one is a camel
foot pattern.

A Home for Everyone?

In some parts of the world there are not enough homes and many people live on the streets or in shanty towns.

As more people leave the countryside and move to the cities the problems become worse.

Our cities need enough homes for all the people who live there. We need to find new ways of living together in future so that everyone has a home.

(Right) Scientists in the USA experiment to find new ways of building cities that will provide enough homes and food for everyone.

(Left) Modern houses can be attractive and cheap to run. We need to build more of them.

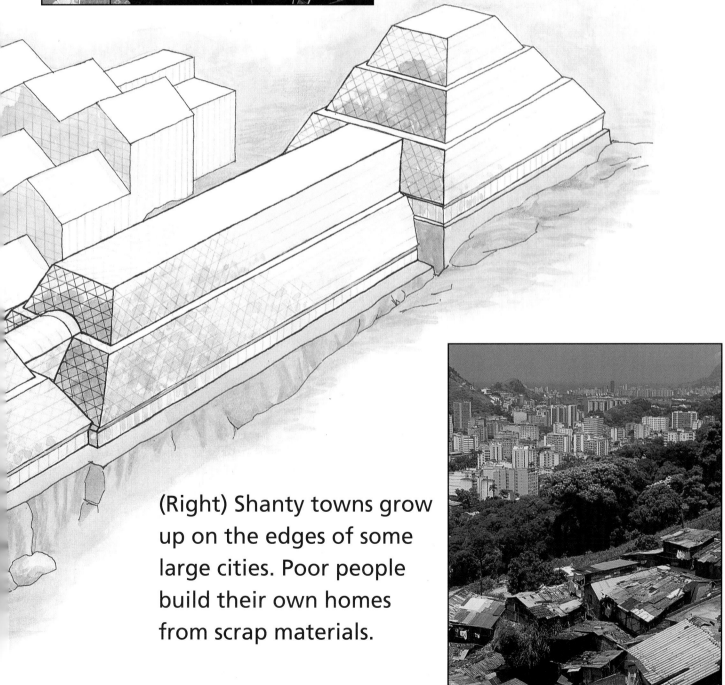

(Right) Shanty towns grow up on the edges of some large cities. Poor people build their own homes from scrap materials.

Word List

Balcony   A small platform with a wall or railing around the upstairs window of a house.

Bamboo   A tree-like grass which grows wild in south-east Asia. The stems are hollow and can be used to make furniture and build homes.

Bark   The tough outer covering of a tree trunk.

Canal   A waterway built by people.

Caravan   A home on wheels that can be moved from place to place.

Caravan site   A place where caravans are parked. This may be for a few nights or for a long time.

City   A large town where thousands of people live and work. Cities are centres for government, business, shopping and trade.

Coal   A solid fuel that can be burned to give heat energy which may be changed into electricity, used to warm homes, or run machinery. Oil and gas are similar fuels except oil is liquid and gas is invisible like air.

Countryside   Land outside the cities and towns which may be farmland, forest, moorland or desert. It may be have hills, mountains or be flat land.

Drains   A network of pipes under the ground through which dirty water from homes passes to special farms where the water is cleaned.

Electricity   Energy that can be used to work machines or provide light and heat.

Flats   A home on one floor which shares a building with a number of other flats.

Gypsies   A travelling people found in Europe and North America, who have their own language and customs.

Moat   A ditch around a castle that was often filled with water.

Monsoon   A wind that blows from the sea to the land in southern Asia. It brings heavy rain.

Panel   A flat piece of material which can be used to make a wall.

Rainforests   Thick forests in tropical areas of the world near to the equator where it rains on most days for part of the time.

Romans   People who were Roman citizens at the time of the Roman Empire.

Steel   A form of iron which has many uses. It makes a strong frame for a tall building.

Town   A place where hundreds of people live and work – a centre for shopping and business.

Veranda   A covered passage around a house that is open to the air on the outer side.

Video camera   A camera which passes images to a TV screen and stores them on video tape.

Finding Out More

Places to Visit

Many houses and homes are open to the public in all areas of the country. Also worth visiting are:

The Building Centre
26 Store Street
London WC1E 2YD

The Design Museum
Shad Thames
London SE1 2YD

The Science Museum
Exhibition Road
London SW7 5BD

Books to Read

History From Photographs: Houses and Homes, K. Cox and P. Hughes, (Wayland, 1995)

Homes, Brian Knapp, (Atlantic Europe, 1994)

Homemade Homes, John Nicholson, (Allen & Unwin, 1994)

Homes in Hot and Cold Places, Simon Crisp, (Wayland, 1994)

Houses and Homes, Alistair Hamilton-MacLaren, (Wayland, 1994)

Houses Around the World, Godfrey Hall, (Wayland, 1995)

Poems about Homes, A. Earl & D. Sensier, (Wayland, 1994)

Timelines: Houses, Fiona Macdonald, (Watts, 1994)

Worldwise: Castles, Francesca Baines, (Watts, 1995)

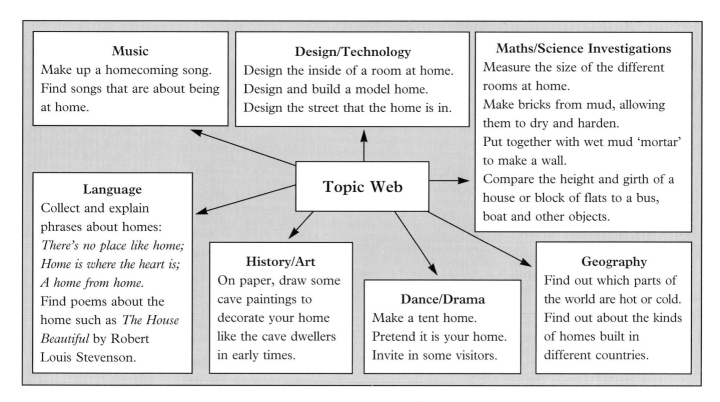

Music
Make up a homecoming song. Find songs that are about being at home.

Design/Technology
Design the inside of a room at home. Design and build a model home. Design the street that the home is in.

Maths/Science Investigations
Measure the size of the different rooms at home.
Make bricks from mud, allowing them to dry and harden.
Put together with wet mud 'mortar' to make a wall.
Compare the height and girth of a house or block of flats to a bus, boat and other objects.

Language
Collect and explain phrases about homes:
There's no place like home;
Home is where the heart is;
A home from home.
Find poems about the home such as *The House Beautiful* by Robert Louis Stevenson.

Topic Web

History/Art
On paper, draw some cave paintings to decorate your home like the cave dwellers in early times.

Dance/Drama
Make a tent home. Pretend it is your home. Invite in some visitors.

Geography
Find out which parts of the world are hot or cold. Find out about the kinds of homes built in different countries.

Index

646